Baby Bed

Brandon Butler

ISBN 979-8-89485-166-2 (Paperback)
ISBN 979-8-89485-167-9 (Digital)

Covenant Books
11661 Hwy 707
Murrells Inlet, SC 29576
www.covenantbooks.com

For Hadley and Beau

12
11
10
9
8
7
6
5
4
3
2
1

Wake up, wake up,
you little sleepy head.
It's time to start the day,
it's time to get out of your baby bed.

To start the day, we'll change your diaper
and get you dressed.
Then we'll feed you,
because a full belly in the
morning is always best.

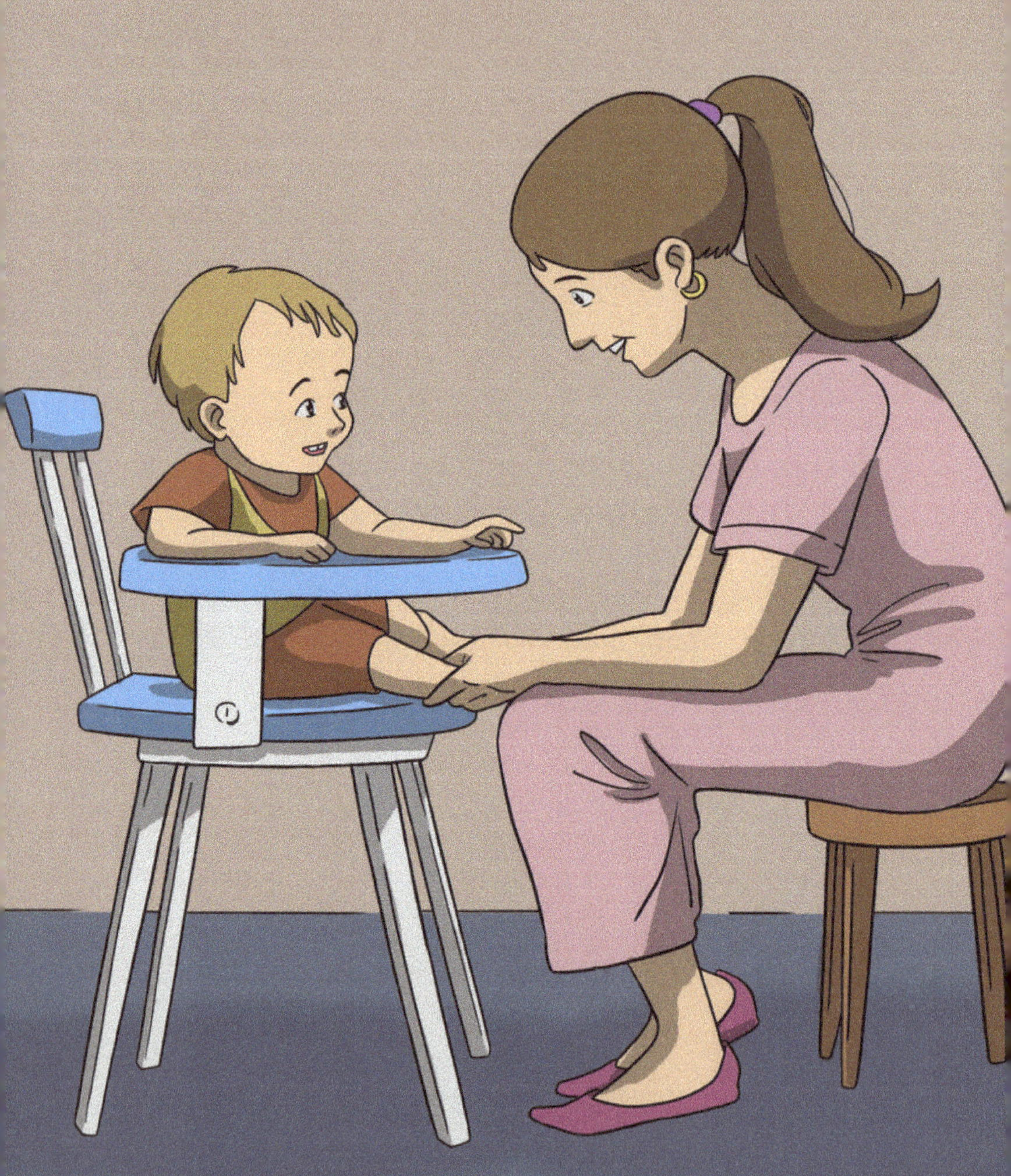

And while you finish eating,
I'll want to close my eyes to think about sleep.
But I'll refrain for now,
instead watching and holding
your tiny little feet.

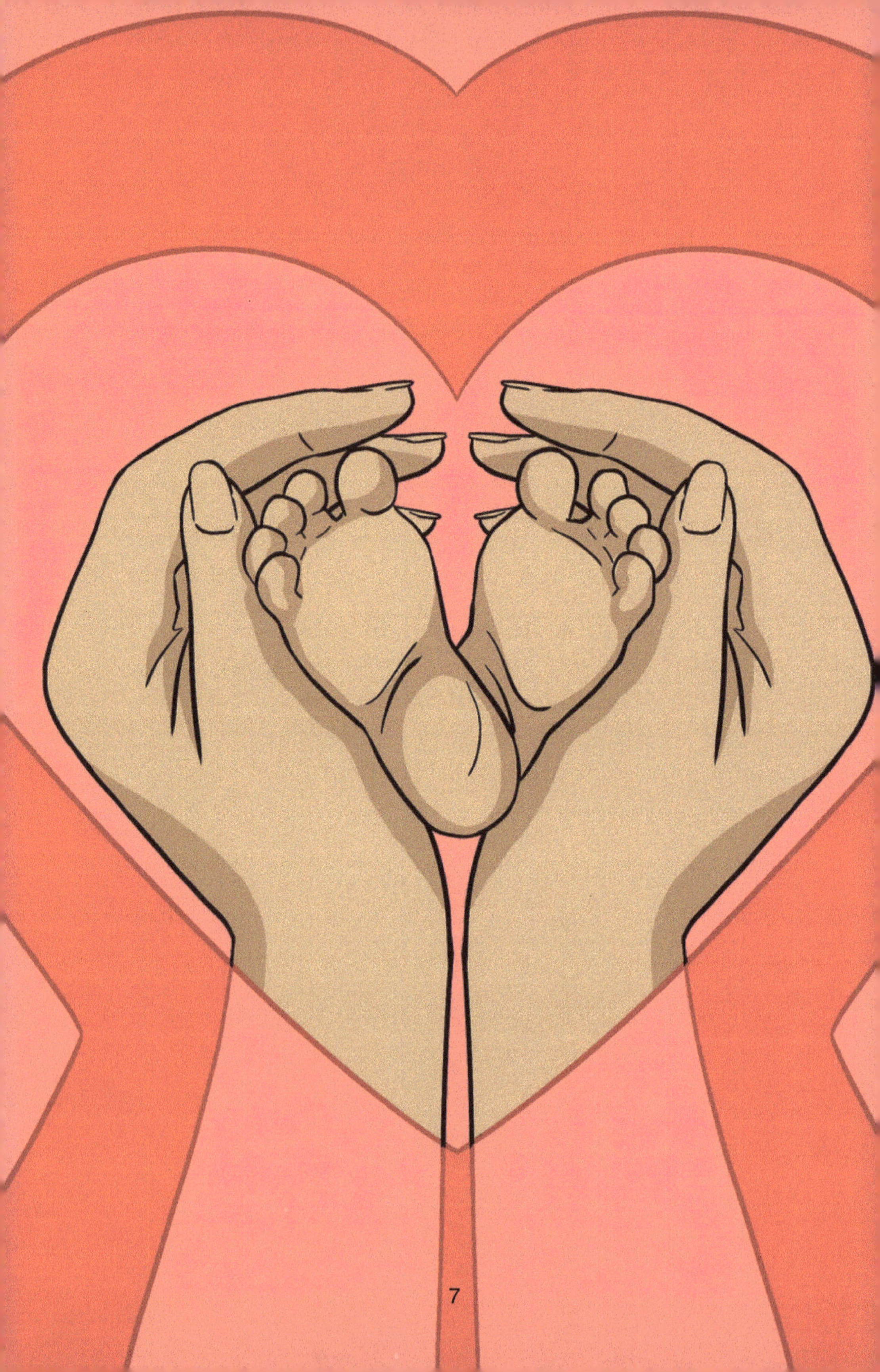

Those tiny little feet, I'll admit,
I adore.
I could hold them all day,
that is one thing for sure.

Then I'll do a few things,
while you play in the living room.
Before too long,
it will be nap time at noon.

When it's your nap time,
I'll lay down as well for a little snooze.
Since I've met you,
sleep is one thing I've begun to lose.

Now the afternoon is gone,
just as quick as it came.
The day is almost over,
and, boy, that's a shame.

Over and over,
the days go so fast.
I think to myself,
as you're in the bath.

Now here we are,
back in the rocking chair.
I feed you your bottle,
as I run my hands through your hair.

Feeding you your bottle,
that's what makes you grow.
Sometimes I don't want to,
because I wish the growing would slow.

So tonight,
I'll hold you tight and kiss your little head.

11 12 1
10 2
9 3
8 4
7 6 5

Because who knows,
this could be the last time I get
to lay you in your baby bed.

About the Author

As a device rep by day and a devoted dad/husband by night, Brandon Butler writes a baby book about making the most of the time with your babies.